Darkness Undone

Elayna Mae Darcy

Magic Key Media

Darkness Undone

Copyright © 2020 Elayna Mae Darcy.

All rights reserved. No part of this publication may be reproduced, distributed, or transmitted in any form or by any means, including photocopying, recording, or other electronic or mechanical methods, without the prior written permission of the publisher, except in the case of brief quotations embodied in critical reviews and certain other noncommercial uses permitted by copyright law.

ISBN: 978-1-7323540-2-9 (Paperback)
ISBN: 978-1-7323540-3-6 (eBook)

Book Design by Elayna Mae Darcy.
Illustrations by Elayna Mae Darcy.
Front Cover Image by Damian A. Falana.

Printing & Distribution by Ingram Spark.

First Edition, October 2020.

Magic Key Media
Philadelphia, PA 19140

*For my father.
I wish you could have
witnessed who I became.*

> "*Even the darkness is not dark to you—*
> *the night is bright as the day,*
> *for darkness is as light with you.*"
>
> **Psalm 139:12**

OTHERS
We walked through shadow.
Your hand in mine, guiding me
to a place called hope.

With Love, Your Story

Dear Storyteller,

>Pen me a promise
>with your ink-stained fingers.
>Promise me you won't
>let my words
>go unsaid.
>
>Pledge to me with your
>loneliness-stained lips
>that you won't
>forget about me,
>that you'll
>tell me to the world
>even if their
>lie-stained ears
>refuse to listen.

Vow to me
you won't let me go
until my adventures
whisk away the
hope-stained hearts
of the readers who
most need to
believe in something
bigger than any of us.

Swear to me
you won't give up on me—
and most importantly—
yourself.

>>With Love,
>>>Your Story

Give The Universe

You have always been
        a bud, fit to bloom
who fought so hard
        through rock & soil
to be here
        with your soft beauty
and handsome bravery
        and inspired brilliance.

Your eyes always fixed
        on outer space, gazing
at other worldly suns.
        But when I look at you,
I see stardust sprung
        up from the ground,
a constellation of
        petals and thorns
to whom I wish
        I could give the
                universe.

The Strangers

They sit huddled
by the fence
speaking words
I cannot hear,
but I like to
imagine they are
marveling at
life's mysteries
with me.

The Poet

Under the moon
& unseen stars
& the evening
Germantown air outside
Uncle Bobbie's bookshop,
I soaked in
the magic and
the hope of
the poet I look
up to the most.

She told me
to tell my story
before anyone
could take it.
She spoke of
choices and dreams
and how to fight
until I'd made it.
She asked the
young people
for their questions
and their art,
and for me,
she lit a fire and
reignited my spark.

The Librarian

No words
could ever fully convey
what a safe haven
you made for me.

In that musty
little library,
you showed me
that *myself* was enough,
that books could be
portals to other worlds
and places for me
to find peace.

With those scribbled
passes to get me out
of homeroom,
you showed me that
strangers could be
kinder than family
and that words
were the most
powerful form of magic.

So much of who I am
was molded in those mornings,
talking with you as
we put away books
and mused about life
in ways that made me
feel more seen than
I'd ever been.

I'll forever carry
that joy you gave me
simply by listening
to my stories and
assuring me they
were worth chasing.

Divine Secrets of the Driveway Sisterhood

We share a tapestry
of memories
woven from midnight summers,
candle wax & pavement,
the smell of
burned paper edges
covered with inscriptions
of deepest wishes.

Feathers and the
dust of crushed geodes
and a broken glass
symbol of the trinity.

That is what you were to me.

A somehow holy
set of sisters, together
in solidarity through
all those high school
trials & uncertainties.

Life led us through fights
where we faced demons, and
I know not everything
that we were then
remains now.
But I've never forgotten
laying on blankets
while we imagined how
life would look
when we grew up.

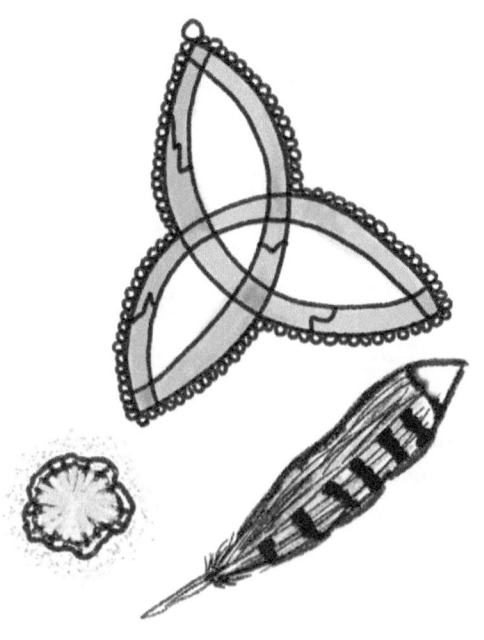

One of you
once said,
"I say this with
stars in my eyes…"
and I've long regretted
that I don't remember
the rest of your sentence.
But those eight words
captured the essence of
our driveway summer
magic,
where we were more
infinite
than anything else
in the world.

Those football field
sunrises by the
middle school
are nestled in my bones,
reminders that when life
gets boring, there is always
something beautiful
in the simple.

That three kids
who started out
strangers
could become sisters
across space
and through time.
That love never breaks,
and teenage hope
never dies.

Soulmates

I used to believe
that soulmates
were singular.
A one-to-one
relationship in everyone's
life, no room
for others—
no chance at
mistakes.

But the more
years I spend here
on this rotating rock,
the more I realize
that our fates
have many faces.

A soulmate
can be a lover,
a mother,
or a friend.

They are the humans
who you find
home in.

Collective Strength

We are so much more
than any employer
said we were.
Our worth never
determined in
the clocked hours
we worked, or how
professionally we
did (or didn't) dress.

In this time of
start-ups & trust funds
we forget that we
are ancient & magnificent
with every element
of Mother Earth
inside of us.

Fire—our passion burning.
Water—our hope like a tide, surging.
Air—our lungs quietly breathing.
Earth—grounding us in meaning.
Ether—free souls, ever being.

We have always been
wonder & worthy
without needing to
ask permission.

Our hearts hold more
value than any salary.
The love within us
more expansive
than galaxies.

A Place Where You Find People

An entire generation
laid out before me
in their revelry,
and I, the fly
on the wall.
The latest seed
to be planted in
the soil of this
community
that has been tended
with hardworking hands
and watered with love.
Husbands & coworkers,
wives & friends,
partners & persons...
so many lives
changed along the way,
all because of
an idea that this
"is a thing we
do together...
a place where
you find people..."

Watch You Go

Here at the
end of all things,
I'm still just
wishing you would
believe in yourself.
Because somehow
in all the things
you were selfish about,
it was never
love or patience
or kindness
for yourself.
I pray that
one day, you
understand
we never wanted
to watch you go,
but we could not
continue to
watch you
eat yourself alive.

The Wrong Family

I wish our blood
meant more,
but I guess it
never did.

The friends I've had
have held my hand
even as you
left me reaching
for empty air.

They helped me
sail safely through
every tempest
life tossed at me,
while you sat
somewhere on a shore,
peacefully pretending
that I was lost
at sea.

Yet still
I long for a day when
I share DNA with
a family who cares,
who understands
and celebrates
just how much love
I have to give.

What You Left Me

In my feelings
but out of body...
soul drifting somewhere
abstract between
then & now,
somewhere still
somehow filled
with all the
hope you left me.

That was my true
inheritance from you,
the kind no
insurance policy
could give or promise.

You left me with
kindness & grit,
with a spirit that
while generous,
never took shit
from anyone.
Fierce love
from a heavy heart,
but one that could still
be light with laughter.
These are the treasures that
no bank account
could ever hope to measure.

Harbor

Maybe I've
moved on from you
the way that
ships move on
from their harbors.
Free and
out to sea,
where adventures
await me,
far away from
the home
you once were
to me...

DEATH
After the breaking,
I learned to stand on my own.
Though still—the pain gnaws.

Now

More than anything,
it is the little things
that I miss.
The walla of
a busy cafe,
the laughter of
children on a
fresh spring day.
In this isolated
and touch-starved now,
all I can miss is
how my friends once hugged me,
how the sun once loved me,
and how peaceful
many voices in a small space
used to sound
before the whole world
went dark & silent.

After Losing You

"Did I dream it?"

The first words
I whispered
the morning after
my world ended.

I Drew Death

I drew Death
from the deck today,
and I don't know
if I really comprehend
what this card
means for me
on a day as
heavy as this.

Perhaps some
part of me must die
so that the rest of me
survives.

Maybe I'm meant
to let you go
so that who I am
can begin to flourish
and grow.

(Ten)ses

This decade
has been a minute.
Somehow I blinked
and there you were
and then I blinked
and there you weren't.
Losing you has been
a ten year yesterday
that I keep wishing
I'd wake up from.

This decade
has been an eternity.
Somehow I grew up
without you in an age
that went on and on
into a tomorrow
you would never see.
Losing you has been
a ten year forever
that I keep wishing
I could sleep through.

Thoughts from the 23

Cobblestones
and broken windows.
Churches
and worn-out soles.
Colors,
brilliant, but the paint peeling.
Catharsis
a commodity these city
corners don't get to have.

Tomorrow?

We said,
"We'll see you tomorrow..."
not knowing if
she had any left.

We crowded
around her, photos
of a life on
the wall,
a curtain
separating out
the world
she once belonged to,
while the remnants
of our family
filled the decaying air
with our joy
and our memories
and a promise of cookies
tomorrow...
the tomorrow that
never came.

On the Train to My Grandmother's Funeral

The sky at sunrise
was cardinal red,
painted with strokes of
orange,
        purple,
                & pink.
The colors are so
alive,
and I want
you to be here
to see them.
To see the birds
soaring against
this morning's
impressionist sky.

As I watch
from the windows
of the train we
used to ride
together when
I was small enough
to sit on your lap,
I take comfort
in believing
that you're up
there in that sky,
painting these
clouds for me to see,
for me to turn into
poetry to remember
the best of you.

There's so much
I learned from you.
Tenacity.
       Grace.
              Faith.

You were never
perfect, but
you were a
person—
one who I loved
and who gave love
and who will be
beloved always.

Somehow, Again

My hands are still shaking,
but I manage
somehow
to pick up the pieces.
To pick up my pen
again,
somehow...

I know one day
I'll drop it
again,
when life gets hard
again.
But I know too
that my shaking hands
will keep writing words
and weaving worlds,
and that I'll be all
the stronger for
surviving

again

somehow...

My Open Letter to the Class of Whenever

My dear graduates, if only you could know what lies ahead. If I could, I would impart that you have only just begun your lives. Your black gowns adorned with colorful accomplishments and the smiles of your families are here to swaddle you into your futures, for while you don't know it yet, today, in a way, you are reborn.

Ahead of you lies forever. There are promises to be kept to make up for all the nights gone unslept in pursuit of knowledge and creativity and growth. Passing cars on Broad Street sound their horns for you, and joyful voices shout to honor your victory. Yet as triumphant as the happy scene makes me, there lingers a bitter melancholy.

Though it does not rain, the sky above us is gray, and I sit before you with my pen knowing that today, one of the students who should be among you tried to take their own life.

Their father should have been happy to watch their child finish their last semester, yet instead, he had to see that child with blood along their neck, a deep and thick cherry red.

I never found out what it was that haunted them enough to make them try to meet their end, but I tell you this so you understand that even this lowest moment was one that they survived. They made it out alive, and lived to know how loved they were, so that they could move forward and try to mend.

All I can hope is that you will keep in your hearts the knowledge that all moments, good and bad, do pass. Even when grades barely made it, there came another chance for you to try again. I hope that no matter what haunts you, you know that today, and every day, is a new beginning. A new opportunity to choose to keep living.

Ode to Peabody Hall

I stand before
empty land where
my most treasured home
one stood.
What once were halls
poured of concrete memories
and stones made of moments
are now only open air
and grass
and dirt that
looks terribly alone
without us.
The basement that
used to be filled
with energy and art
is now buried, along with
a piece of my heart.
This hallowed ground,
once filled with
sounds of joy and
heartache and
togetherness
at all hours,
now only a vacant lot
where flowers grow
in the shadow of
our misfit home,
where we sang
about finding love
in a hopeless place.

Ache of an Ember

How much must
an ember ache
in its final moments,
becoming ash?

And how free must
an ember feel
blossoming back,
a phoenix, at last?

Then

I no longer
      fear oblivion,
because I have learned
      that it doesn't exist.

I used to believe
that *this* was all there was,
but life and her lessons
have shown me there is more
beyond the expiration dates
our bodies have stamped
on all of our atoms.

      Out there and after *this*
           there is a freedom from form
                and a place where I will not
                      need to change who I am
                            just to belong.

HEARTBREAK

You didn't need me.
Turns out, I didn't need you.
I needed myself.

Gone, But Not...

The place where we met
doesn't exist anymore,
the memories we
made there not enough
to hold the brick and mortar
together in the
face of change.

The hardest truth
to swallow is that
we don't exist
anymore either.

They say every
seven years,
your body becomes
entirely new.
Every cell of you
regenerates.
If that's true,
then there's nothing
left of me or
of you or
the place we
first began.

I hope that
means that the
next time I
see you,
we'll get to start over,
and become
something new
that won't be
forgotten.

It's Just Science

The space/time continuum
never had anything on
the power of
our chemistry,
physics bending us
toward one another
against astronomical
odds and the chemical
imbalances that
leave me feeling
so trapped in
my own mind.

I know you
to be a student of science,
but believe me when
I say there is a
magic and
artistry
connecting us
that no lab could explain.

Humans are
limited, yes,
but I must confess
that to me,
you're the one
celestial being
I'd break all
the rules for,
because my soul knows
that the two of us
are meant for more.

#Hope

Your upside-down smile
and your thumbs up
and your tears of joy
were just what
my sparkling heart
needed
to know
there might still
be #hope for us...

Starbound

I don't know if
I can do this again...
be in orbit
around someone who
doesn't look up
at the sky and
see me drifting...
I need someone
with eyes always
starbound
if ever I'm to
hear the words,
"I love you too..."

If You're Reading This...

Eyes shut
but heart open,
I imagine you're
right here and
right now and
your fingers are
tracing my lips
to where my smile
meets my eyes.

You're close enough
that soon your hands
run over my thighs,
falling in love with
every inch of me,
because everyone
before you said
there was too much
of me to ever
be beautiful.

I wish that
right here and
right now, your
mouth is only
a breath away and
that your tongue
is tasting mine,
and you're so close
that not even time
could fill the space
between us.

I know you aren't
really here,
that this is all
only a dream,
but if the day ever
comes when you are
in my arms,
maybe this poem
is one I'll let
you read.

Rooms of You

That effortless way
your laughter
wraps around me
fills me up
with as much
warmth as a
living room hearth.
It feels easy,
existing with you,
like sitting on a
wraparound porch
breathing fresh
air from the sea.
And when you
become quiet and
vulnerable,
I feel
like you're opening
a door and inviting
me in,
saying that I am worthy
of dwelling here
with you in these
rooms of you that
not everyone
is allowed to see.

Stay?

You kept the card
that I gave you close,
so it could bring you
some sun on your
rainiest days.

Why couldn't you
have kept the
rest of me close
and asked for
me to stay?

Whispered Name

Did you hear me
whispering your name
to the paper
in the middle
of the night?
Did my lovestruck verses
visit your dreams
so that when you
woke up, you were
thinking of me?
Maybe there's more
to this—to us—
than I dared imagine.
Maybe waiting for us
is a happily ever after all.

(Im)Perfect (Poetry)

this haiku is not (perfect)
but darling, neither are we
doesn't mean we're not (poetry)

Waiting For A Train

Too often
have I been
the lonely traveler,
waiting on
the empty platform
for trains
and loves
that never come.

Sometimes
a fellow traveler
runs up,
just in time
to board their
train to some other
destination where I
can't follow.

My train feels
eternally delayed,
so late that
I wonder if
it will ever
come at all.

We Were More Than Things

There was so much
meaning attached
to these arbitrary objects.

The box of matches
from that bar
we stayed
too late at.
The texts that said,
love you so much!
(even when you didn't)
The photos of us
drunk & stumbling—
smiling when we still
had reasons to.

With every
remnant of you
I get rid of,
I become more of
a stranger to myself,
struggling to relearn
who I thought I was.

I must become
someone new
outside of who
I was with you.

With every belonging
that goes into the bin
the more I begin
to realize that
it was the memories
that really made
us.

We were the
late night talks
and cover band concerts
and the cigarette breaks
I took with you,
even though
I never smoked.

We weren't any
of these physical things,
we were the
moments shared,
the things I couldn't
throw away,
even if I wanted to.

Non-Binary

The only binary thing
about us was that
we were two stars
caught up in
each other's
orbit,
where love was
our only gravity.

no ink left

i'm filling up
pages and pages
not even caring
to be bothered
with punctuation
because with you
there's no question marks
and you make me
feel like one long
run-on thought
that i never want
to end
i want you to
be the sentence
the paragraph
the friend
that i keep loving
even when there's
no ink left
in my pen

Tiny, Infinite Organs

Geodes are most
beautiful when
broken open,
shattered,
hearts laid bare.
In this state
we see all that
always was glittering
inside of them.

Maybe human hearts
are the same...
only after we've broken
can we know what
infinite glory these
tiny organs have
been holding.

DESTROY
*All the words you used
against me became kindling.
I burned down the lies.*

A Long Time to Grow

I'll never be
sorry enough
for all the sorrys
I shouldn't have said,
all the apologies
I made for existing.
All the times
my mind made me
believe that I
was the core
of every wrong
in the world.

I hope you know
I'm trying, even
though you think
there is only *do*
or *do not*.

Maybe doing and being
are like the creation
of the cosmos—
a big bang
that takes a
few billion years
to become.

It might not
look like I'm changing,
but beneath the
sobbing panic attacks,
plates are shifting
soil is forming
and new life
is readying to

break through
and show you
I can become
the person you
always knew I was.

You taught me
about the Spirit
and its fruits,
and while I know
you think it's taking
too long a time,
I promise
the hope in me
has roots
and I believe
soon will be
a season for
blooming.

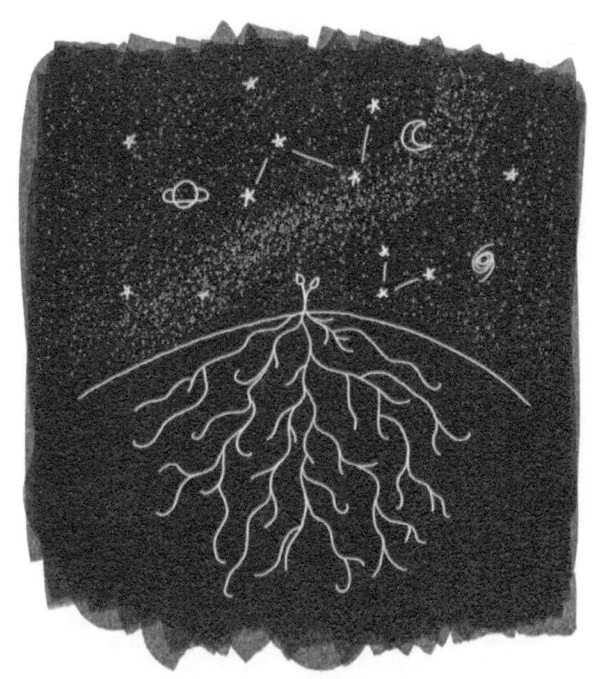

Not This Time

Doubt is
the demon
of the day.
But it cannot
defeat me.
Not when I
have something
to say...

Punished

My healing has come from
taking every feeling
that punishes me
and leaving it
alone to starve.

Wake of Ruin

The fear that
my thoughts don't
matter to anyone
has splintered my
fingers, and for years
that fear kept
        my pen still
                my mouth shut
                       my spirit broken.

But poetry
helped me lay
r
 u
  i
   n
to the notion
that I have nothing
of value to say.

Hope ate the fear
leaving only
confidence in its
w
 a
  k
   e.

My Space

I know that
I don't always
neatly fit
into seats,
or your boxes,
or your impossible
expectations.
But I take up
the space I'm
meant to,
and whether or not
there is any of me
that might be lost
or gained,
there will never
be an inch of me
that you get to
tell me doesn't
deserve to exist.

To All the Day Jobs I Had Before

They thought by
planting me in a cage
they could
choke out my
roots, turn me
into a plastic
succulent like
the rest of them.

They didn't expect
me to fight back.

Through the bars
of my cage, I
blossomed anyway.
My weak
but unrelenting
vines spindled up
to soak in
every drop of
sun and rain
they could reach.

I've grown stronger here,
through every fear that
I wasn't tough enough
and that one day
I might just give up.

But I broke through
and my branches bloom
freely now
because no matter how
much they tried to
stifle me,
I never gave up
my will to be.

That cage lies broken
and all that remains
are the scars
of the bars
that once tried
to stop me.

At last,
I'm free to
grow deep into
the soil
and spread
seeds of hope
in those gardens
that Lin-Manuel said
I'd never get to see.

Inkblood

*"Take those pens
out of your hair!"*

*"Don't draw
on your skin!"*

Phrases my teachers
yelled at me,
not knowing my
insides are made
of ink.

They think
they can take
my stories
from my grasp,
but the last thing
I'll ever let
anyone do
is take my words
away from me.

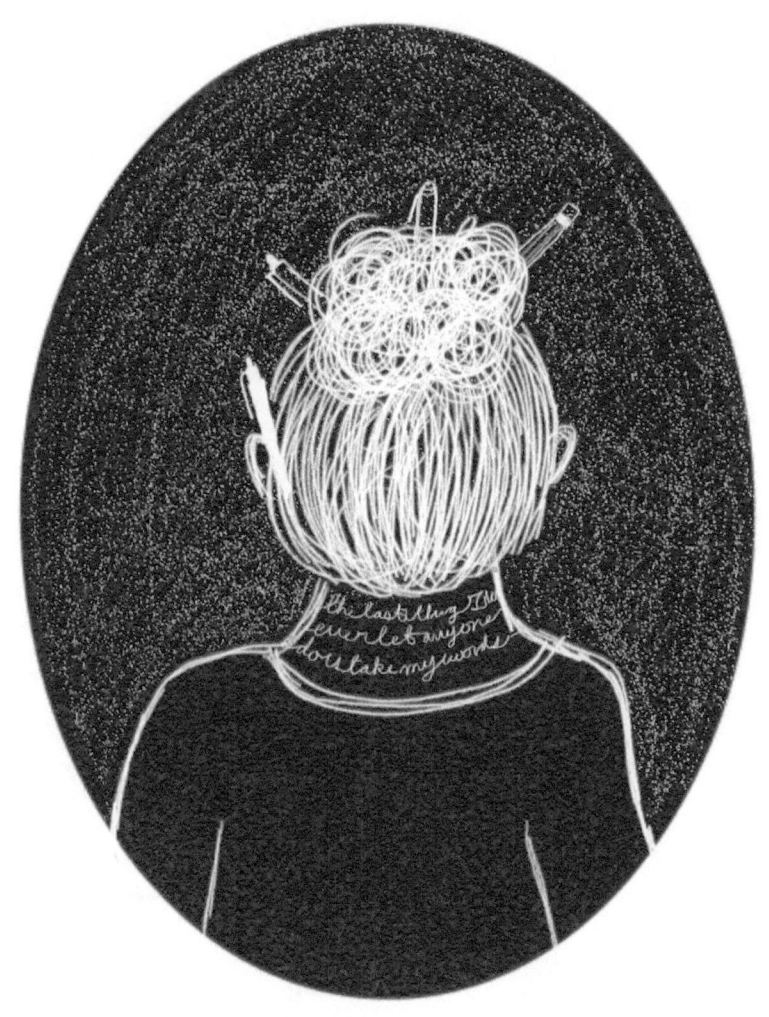

Reclaiming My Time

Time crawls
for me now,
these days that
belong entirely to me
still in their infancy
as I relearn
how to be a
person first.

For so long
I was a servant to
someone else's watch,
beholden to that
office clock.
Expected to fake
my smiles and treat
the client like
a spoiled child
to whom everyone
must bend the knee.

Now,
my time is
mine again,
and I think
I forgot what
that freedom
felt like.
Perhaps I never
truly knew it
at all.

In my early life
I was too small to
fend for myself.
In the classroom,
I became a
statistic that
no one believed
would amount to much.
In the workforce,
surrounded by tasks
and commands,
no real encouragement
to keep learning or growing.

Now,
I'm starting over.
Humanity rebooted.
Existence reloaded.

I'm a once and future
and always queen
who belongs to
and answers to
no one but
my own heart.

Warrior Queen

My kindness
used to make me feel
like a princess who
had been locked
away in a tower
because no one
wanted to deal with
the soft-hearted,
too-sensitive
damsel in
depression.

But the more I grow,
the more I know
my kindness
makes me a warrior queen
who will not be
locked away forever.

My kindness
is fierce and loud,
and nevertheless,
persists.

So try and lock it up,
but my kindness
will never give in
so long as it lives
in a world full of
people worth
fighting for.

Mothers of Tomorrow

I think the day is coming
where we will be able to
let go of the traumas
that our own mothers
laced into our veins.

I believe we can become the
generation of mothers who
do not pick apart their children,
and who will love them in
all the ways that they exist.

REMAIN

*In my darkness, I
discovered how to endure.
I exist in joy.*

Seasons of Me

I'm unsure
on this uneven
late summer morning.
Can I let go of
my many ghosts,
or will they forever
cling to me
like fallen leaves
to the ground?

Autumn is coming,
and with it,
a season of dying
where summer promises
wash out to sea.
But maybe this
dying season
can be different.

Maybe those
fallen leaves can
take my hauntings
out to the gutter
so that by the time
the death and snow
of winter settles,
I'll be left only
with the seeds of me
that can bloom
back to life
in the rebirth
of spring.

Broad Street Line

Blurs of burning-out
tungsten lamps amid
shadow-soaked tunnels.

Pillars.
Lights.
Pillars.
Lights.
A sign of something.

Quick glimpses
of curious sun and sky
peeking through grates
that sometimes run
with rain.

This underground
passage is an
infinite mirror,
reflecting back
the darkness
of broken systems.

But look closer
at the reflections
in the thick windows
and behold
glimmers of hope
in the eyes of those
about to leave
this gathering place
and emerge into
the light of day.

No One Can See

Authenticity
is a complicated journey
to be gentler with
yourself.
It isn't always
pins or badges or pride flags...
sometimes it's staring
down the mirror
and seeing all that
is worth loving
within you.
Even when our
societies and bodies
betray us,
our hearts are
a pulsing reminder,
a thrumming truth
that no one can see
the reasons inside
that keep you existing.

Magnificent Mess

I am kind of
a mess, but that's
what makes me
magic.
When did you
ever see a spell
that was clean
and pretty?
I am the mashed-up
rose petals and the
ashes of incense.
I am the sparks
from matchboxes
and old letters getting
frayed at the edges.
I'm the glint of
moonlight on
waters dark and deep.
I'm the most
magnificent mess
that you will
ever meet.

Multitudes

Not even
the Mariana Trench
is deep enough
to contain
my multitudes.

Travel to
the moon or Mars
and still, by far,
my imagination
reaches on
and on
and on.

More sprawling
than the stars,
untameable
as the seas,
my imagination
is the glorious
most infinite
part of me.

She Doesn't Care

The sun on a beautiful day
does not care how much
you are hurting,
or that you feel broken.
She shines and smiles down
on you anyway, in hopes
that for a moment,
you might smile too.

Eclipse

When fear rises
and eclipses hope,
remember
that hope is
an ever burning light
and fear is
no more than
a passing shadow.

Don't Worry

Galaxies don't worry
that they take up
too much space,
nor are flowers bothered
by how long they
take to bloom.
So why then
do you apologize
for the time it takes
to become you?

Careful Magic

When I see birds
and blossoms of
every color, I truly
have to wonder
how anyone could
ever look upon
the cosmos
and see something
random and unplanned?

Our cells look
like universes.
Our arms share
the same veins
as flower petals,
and the light of
the sun in our eyes
is the same as the
stars in distant skies.

How could a life
filled with so much
careful magic
be nothing more
than tragic and
untempered chaos?

Be Alive

I'm learning
to be patient
with myself.
I'm remembering
to breathe
and take the time
to taste the
sweet cream in
my coffee like
it's a kind word
to my tastebuds.
I'm trying
to let go of
the pain that
adds weight to
my days that
need not be there.
I'm loving the
dazzle in my
own eyes when I
catch them in
the mirror
in the morning.
I'm smiling
because I realize
I should feel
blessed to just
be alive.

Human's Guide For Not Giving Up

First,
you must remember
what a treasure
you are.
Remember all the
microscopic ways
that the atoms
of the universe
conspired in order
to make you.

Then,
remember
how loved you are.
That someone,
somewhere in this chaotic
cosmos we call home,
loves all of you
and thinks of you
the way you do
your favorite song.

And last,
but never least,
remember that
even the most mundane
of your days is
an adventure you
have been called to.
That if you are still here,
despite every reason
you think you shouldn't be,
it is because whatever destiny
fate has in store for you
isn't finished yet.

Arrival

I think I've
been waiting for an
arrival—
a moment when
all my dreams & wantings
become tangible things
I can hold in my hands
and hug to my chest,
instead of just being
a pulsing, hoping
abstraction that
beats inside of me.

The problem, of course,
is that an
arrival
implies stopping.
Getting off the bus
because we reached
our destination.

An arrival
indicates a journey's end,
but neither we
nor our art
are finite.
With final pen strokes
begins the life of the work
that lives on long
after we've gone
back to the stardust
we were molded from.

Perhaps it's time
I remembered that an
arrival
is not what I should
be searching for.
Maybe it is
the adventure
I should enjoy living
while I still
have the chance.

∞ ∞ ∞

Special Thanks

This is the part where I get to shout out the remarkable folks who helped bring this book to life during the initial Kickstarter campaign in the spring of 2020. Crowdfunding is such a wild journey, made all the more wild by taking place during a global pandemic, but all of you who contributed were beacons of hope during that dark time. Thank you so much for supporting these poems.

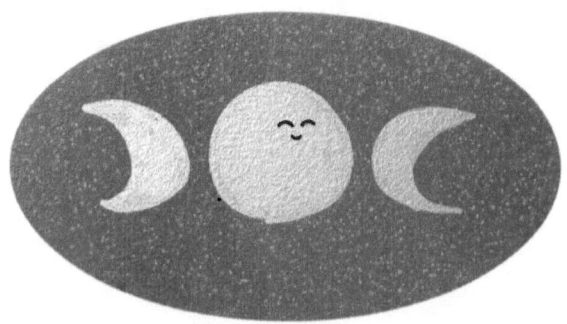

***Darkness Undone* Kickstarter Backers**
Anaia Daigle
Anonymous
Ashley Craig
Ashley Sousa
Beth Warsaw
Brittney Morris
Cheyenne Williamson
Chrissy Tomilson
Elan Samuel
Megan Congdon
Pam Selle
Peak Johnson
Robyn White
Sharon Henry
Sushi
Tal M. Klein
Taylor Shuster
Trisha Swed

Acknowledgements

To Ari... my dear friend, my wise frond, my fearless editor who taught me to use indentation with reckless abandon—this book wouldn't exist without you. From early morning texts to all day word sprints to adventures in Old City, your generosity of spirit inspires the shit out of me. Thank you for your careful edits and your all caps lock encouragements. You are a masterful wordsmith and such a professional feels dealer, and my life would sincerely suck without you in it. Thank you for being.

To Brittney... I am so glad to have met you and to have you in my life, and can't thank you enough for how much you have lifted me up and reminded me that my joy is worth protecting, and my words worth fighting for.

To Alicia... the way in which you have shared my words with others and shown me so much support since my first book's debut will never be forgotten. Whenever I am doubting myself, I think, "what would Alicia say?" because I know you'd find some way to encourage me. You are a gift, my dear.

To Alex, Adam, and Anaia... I wrote a whole book and yet there are no words I can write to thank you enough for the joy y'all have brought into my life through Indy Hall. When I felt aimless and like I might never be good enough, you and so many other folks within our community lifted me up and helped me find the courage to chase my dreams more fully than I ever had before. Many of these poems were scribbled in the walls of the Hall on Market Street, and none of that would have happened were it not for your kindness. The JFDI philosophy is one I'll carry with me forever, and it's a huge reason this book exists.

To Damian and Jay... thank you both for pushing me all these years. For supporting me. For loving me, even in ways I couldn't always understand. For games of Catan and Mario Kart when I needed a break. I love you both so much and I am so grateful to call you my friends. I cannot wait for the world to know your stories as I do.

And to any and everyone who has read both or either part of this duology... I hope you have enjoyed my words as much as I enjoyed getting to share them with you. Please friend, never give up on yourself.

About the Author

Elayna Mae Darcy (she/they) is a queer poet, YA author, and filmmaker who just has a lot of feelings. A proud Philadelphian, Elayna has a passion for engaging with fandom communities, and has written articles, produced podcasts, and spoken on panels across the country. With a head in the clouds and heart in the stars, Elayna is the author of the sci-fi short story, CONTINUUM (2017), and the poetry collection, UNRAVELING LIGHT (2018). Most days they can be found scribbling stories in cafes or wandering about Philly with their camera in hand.

elaynamusings.com

twitter | @elaynamae
instagram | @elaynamusings
tumblr | elaynamusings.tumblr.com
facebook | facebook.com/elaynamusings

www.ingramcontent.com/pod-product-compliance
Lightning Source LLC
Chambersburg PA
CBHW021127080526
44587CB00012B/1166